551.3 Radlauer, Ruth
RAD
       The power of ice

$11.95

DATE			

THE POWER OF ICE

By
Ruth Radlauer and Lisa Sue Gitkin

Photographs by Lisa Sue Gitkin

A Radlauer Geo Book

AN ELK GROVE BOOK

 CHILDRENS PRESS, CHICAGO

**Created for Childrens Press
by Radlauer Productions, Incorporated**

The authors are grateful to Dr. Maynard M. Miller, Dean of the
School of Mines, University of Idaho, and Dr. Ernest Rich,
Professor Emeritus of Geology, Stanford University, California,
for authentication of the manuscript.

To Allan Gitkin

Also to Ray and Virginia Garner and the Associates of the
Idyllwild School of Music and the Arts, who brought us together.

Cover:
Matterhorn, Swiss Alps

Library of Congress Cataloging in Publication Data

Radlauer, Ruth, 1926—
    The power of ice.
    (A Radlauer geo book)
    "An Elk Grove book."
    Includes index.
    Summary: A description of an expedition to explore a
glacier in Alaska introduces facts about glaciers,
including their origin, types, and effects on the earth.
    1. Glaciers—Juvenile literature.   2. Glaciers—
Alaska—Juneau Region—Juvenile literature. [1. Glaciers.
2. Glaciers—Alaska]   I. Gitkin, Lisa Sue. II. Title.
III. Series.
GB2403.8.R33 1985   551.31   85-5714
ISBN 0-516-07839-9

1 2 3 4 5 6 7 8 9 10 11 12 13 14 15 R 91 90 89 88 87 86 85

CONTENTS

This mighty river of snow is only one of many that attracted us to Alaska's Juneau **Icefield**. We're here to explore the mysteries of their presence and power.

SNOWY JULY

Imagine yourself in the middle of July, all bundled up in six layers of clothing. Everything you need to survive is strapped to your back in a huge 60-pound **backpack**. There are ten of us. I'm Bob, the **trail party** leader, and you and I are with five other young people and three scientists who have been skiing across a blizzardy **glacier** for the past four hours.

The snow is coming down harder now. The whole world seems to be one big white blur. I announce that we have ten more miles to ski until we reach the next camp, but neither you, I, nor the other people of our party are sure in which direction we should travel. The hour is late and everyone is cold and tired. Still, because of the midnight sunset, we have enough light to keep going.

It's time to check in with **base camp**, and we stop to get out the walkie-talkie radio. "Base camp, this is Bob's trail party checking in. Come in please."

They advise us to proceed to camp, using compasses and maps to guide us there. The group groans. As the party leader, it's my responsibility to encourage everyone. We have to keep our minds off our aches and pains and continue our trek across this blizzard-ridden glacier of Alaska's Juneau **Icefield**.

backpack	large, compartmented bag held on a sturdy frame to carry sleeping bag and other camping equipment
trail party	group of people out on the trail away from camp for any purpose
glacier	mass of ice with limited width and direction of movement
base camp	station where groups can live temporarily and go out to explore and/or do research
icefields	large areas of land covered by different glaciers and areas of snow and ice accumulation

Everyone in the group groans. We readjust our heavy loads and continue toward base camp.

THE POWER OF ICE

When stomachs growl, someone suggests a dinner break. A cheer goes up and we dig through our packs to find food. You find yours quickly. It's a peanut butter and jelly sandwich that you accidentally sat on during the last rest stop.

We huddle together for warmth and become quietly involved in our own thoughts. I wonder if my faraway friends spent the day at the beach. You mumble something about what your family had for dinner thousands of miles to the southeast. I think about reaching camp safely and then someone asks, "What in the world are we doing here?"

We're here on the Juneau Icefield because we're fascinated by these mighty rivers of ice called *glaciers*. The study of glaciers involves all kinds of scientists: **physicists, chemists, geologists**, and even **botanists**. You and I and the younger members of the group were lucky enough to be chosen as research assistants to 30 scientists who have gathered here from all over the world. We travel on these glaciers, listen to lectures about them, and perform various research projects to further our knowledge of this awesome and hostile environment. Together we're discovering, day by day, the *power of ice*.

physicist   scientist who studies matter, energy, motion, force, and the laws of nature that affect how things work

chemist   scientist who studies properties of substances, how they are put together, and how they react with each other

geologist   earth scientist; one who studies the earth and the rocks of which it is formed

botanist   scientist who studies plants

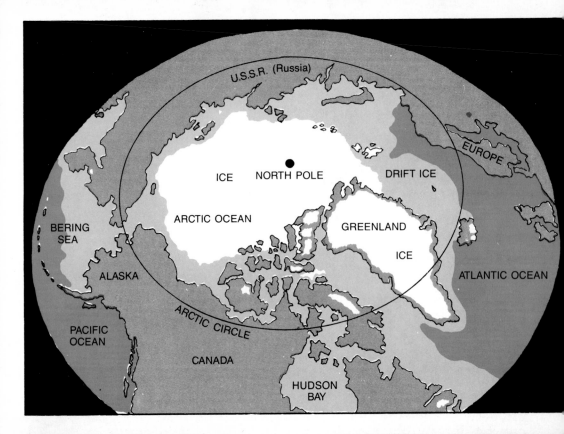

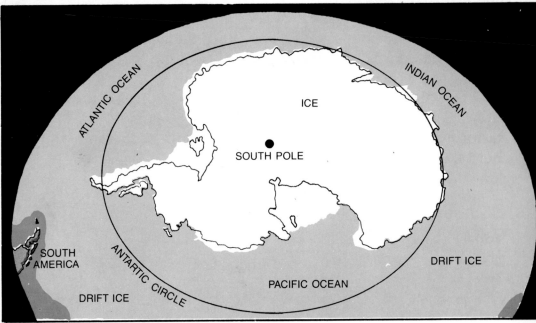

These maps show most of the present ice-covered areas of the world.

WHY STUDY GLACIERS?

I've always been fascinated by the power of ice. Even as we sit here and eat our so-called dinner, I know the ice we're on is moving, but so slowly that we can't see its movement. Yet its power is carving the earth beneath it. Most people don't know how important it is to study these master carvers of some of the earth's landscape.

Glaciology helps us plan for the future and better understand the past. Over three-fourths of the world's fresh water is frozen into glacier ice. The melting of that ice can be a source of water for cities and farm irrigation. Dams in Washington state, Switzerland, and Norway generate **hydroelectric power** for cities by using the force of rivers of **meltwater** from nearby glaciers.

On the other hand, uncontrolled meltwater often causes floods that destroy villages and farms in countries like Peru. If all the glaciers of the world melted, the sea level would rise. Important cities like Boston, London, Sidney, Shanghai, and Peking could be completely under water.

Glaciologists spend long days and nights on these frozen fields, "reading" the ice in search of clues to the history of world climates. Weather trends of the past help us predict future climatic conditions.

drift ice	ice on water broken up by winds and currents
glaciology	study of glaciers
hydroelectric power	electricity generated by the force of flowing water
meltwater	any water melted from snow or ice
glaciologist	scientist who studies glaciers

A glacier is a large natural body of moving ice. It's hard to imagine that these huge icy rivers are actually moving. We can't even see or feel the movement beneath us.

TO KNOW A GLACIER

After eating, we begin to ski again. There's a blister forming on my big toe. I try to ignore it by discussing glaciers with you. What are they? Is a glacier like the ice on freezer walls, or the snow on city streets? Why do ice and snow accumulate in such great amounts in some places and not in others? And how and why do glaciers move and change the face of the earth as they move?

A glacier is defined as a large body of moving ice that has been formed and compacted on land. I like to compare glaciers with a lump of mashed potatoes sitting on a plate. When you dump large spoonfuls right in the center, one on top of the other, the sides spread out and the potatoes underneath get squashed. This is what happens to a glacier.

An area of land gets covered by a lot of snow in the winter. But because there's a lot and because the temperature stays cold in this area, the snow never fully melts. The next winter's snow falls, and like the added mashed potatoes, squashes the snow underneath. The **force of gravity** on tons of snow squeezes air out of the snow crystals, and a thick mound of ice and snow is formed. With each new snowfall, the icy mass gets thicker. Gravity forces it to start spreading out the way the mashed potatoes did. Once it begins to spread, it is considered a glacier.

force of gravity   attraction of bodies toward the center of the earth

The two small glaciers on this mountainside are *hanging glaciers*. Like *alpine* glaciers, their paths follow pre-existing depressions in the face of the rock.

GLACIER TYPES

As we ski and talk, the wind dies down and no longer gives us an idea of the direction we're moving. The lead skier stops to take a **compass bearing**. In this **whiteout** we can't see more than ten feet, so our compasses and maps are our only guides.

We start skiing again, and Matthew, the geologist, disagrees with my mashed potatoes idea. He points out that the earth isn't flat like a plate. It has valleys where winter snow collects and gets thicker, compacting into ice in its thickest regions. When this ice is thick enough, it starts to move very slowly down the valley path. The result is not like mashed potatoes on a plate. Instead, it's an *alpine* or *valley glacier* that looks much like a giant river of ice creeping along. These are the types of highland valley glaciers that make up the Juneau Icefield.

Sometimes there's so much snow and so little summer melting that the valleys become completely filled. Entire plains and mountain ranges can be covered by a huge **ice sheet** or **icecap**. This ice is often as thick or thicker than the height of the Empire State Building and covers large parts of entire continents. Enormous **continental glaciers** like these cover Antarctica and Greenland.

compass bearing	reading of a compass; needle points north and helps you determine which way you want to go
whiteout	weather condition in which you are actually standing in clouds on the snow and you can't see where you are
ice sheet	See *continental glacier*
icecap	constant, dome-shaped covering of ice and snow, especially those at the North and South Poles
continental glacier	ice sheet that covers a large part of a continent and moves out in all directions from a central region of accumulation

Agassiz of Switzerland was among the first scientists who realized that landforms like the Matterhorn in the Swiss Alps were carved by glaciers.

HOW DO WE KNOW?

Amy skis up and joins our conversation. She's a *dendrochronologist*, a botanist who gathers ancient tree remnants that were picked up, carried away, and preserved by the glacier. She then studies them in a laboratory. A chemical analysis tells her the age of the tree and hence the age of the ice that overrode and killed it. The different widths of the tree rings give details of the changing climates when the tree was alive.

Yesterday, Amy spoke to our group about the history of glaciology. She said that for many years, scientists in Europe wondered why some places are covered with strange, **unsorted soils** and truck-size boulders of rock types from faraway places. Some thought they were transported by a huge flood. In the early 1800s, Lyell of Scotland guessed that huge **icebergs** had rafted the soils and boulders far from their source areas and deposited them.

By 1834 a young Swiss scientist, Louis Agassiz, had found enough clues to realize that glaciers from the Alps were responsible for the depositions. During a trip to the U.S., he recognized similar features that American geologists believed to be from a great flood. After examining these features, Agassiz **hypothesized** that these areas, like those in Europe, were once covered by tremendous glaciers. Scientists were just beginning to understand the incredible power of ice and how it has shaped much of the earth on which we live today.

unsorted soils soils composed of mixtures of rock sizes from clays to gravels

iceberg huge mass of ice broken from a glacier, often found floating in water

hypothesize give ideas as possible explanations of something

15

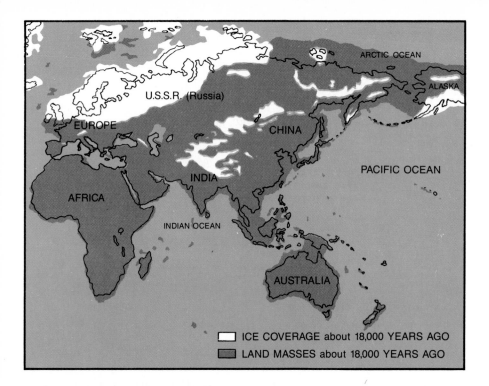

During the Great Ice Age, almost a third of the earth's land was covered with ice during four different periods.

Now scientists believe that 11 different major **ice ages** have occurred during the earth's 4.6 billion-year history. The last major ice age was no more than 11,000 years ago. Scientists call this period of time in the earth's history the *Great Ice Age*. They believe there were four periods of intense cold during the Great Ice Age, when over a third of the earth's land was covered by glaciers. Areas covered were large parts of northern Europe and Asia, southern South America, and much of North America as far south as Kansas and Nebraska.

Between these four **glaciations** were three warming periods when the great ice sheets melted away from the major continents. Some scientists argue that the Great Ice Age is not over yet, and that we're in a fourth warming period.

Today, only 10 percent of the earth is covered by ice, most of which is found around the North and South Poles. One fifth of the states in the U.S. have glaciers. In Alaska there are over 17,000 square miles of ice. The icefields along the coast of Alaska comprise the world's fourth largest ice-covered area. Glaciers are also found on the high mountain ranges of Europe, Asia, South America, and even the highest peaks in Africa.

As Amy and I continue our discussion of the history of glaciology, you ski up behind us and remind me that it's time for another radio check. With groans of relief, we all take off our heavy packs and drop down beside them in the snow. I get out the radio: "Camp 10! Camp 10! This is Bob's trail party, come in please."

ice age   span of geologic time, usually 1—3 million years, when the earth has had alternating warm and cold climates and been alternately covered and uncovered by glaciers—See *Great Ice Age*, page 44.

glaciations   growth and outward spreading of glaciers over a period of time

(top) Both of these glaciers show how *medial moraines* form where two smaller glaciers join. The larger glacier in the center of the picture also shows how much **debris** can accumulate at the *terminus* of a glacier.

(bottom) *Glacial flour* colors meltwater in streams and lakes.

LANDFORMS

While I wait for a radio answer, I see two familiar, jagged peaks through a slight clearing in the clouds ahead of us. They're the Taku Towers, and that means we're not very far from camp. Even though it's 10:30 P.M., we're so far north that the sun won't set before midnight.

I speak into the radio microphone. "Camp 10, we'll be there in about an hour." At camp, Robin responds, "Trail party, roger on that. We'll have the soup good and hot. This is Camp 10 going clear."

The group is excited now and full of energy. We point our skis toward the Towers. Those sharp peaks and jagged ridges are real reminders of the power of ice. The bases of these peaks are still being carved. Many such peaks appear in areas where there are no longer any glaciers. Glaciers of the Great Ice Age deeply **eroded** the landscape wherever they traveled.

How does a glacier like the one we're skiing across erode the solid earth beneath it?" It moves along, powerfully scraping, plucking, and grooving the bedrock. Like a gigantic, non-stoppable earthmover, the glacier erodes a valley, gouging out and leaving behind *glacial drift*, a mixture of rocks, boulders, and finely ground dust. The dust, or *glacial flour*, makes streams and rivers look milky and colors lakes a beautiful turquoise.

Mounds of drift left by a glacier are called *moraines*. The ones left at the sides are called *lateral moraines*. Those at the front of the glacier, or the *terminus*, are called *terminal moraines*. Where two glaciers come together, they form a *medial moraine*, sometimes as wide as a two-lane highway.

debris loose fragments of rock, earth, and other materials
erode wear away

Switzerland's Matterhorn was formed by the power of ice. It is
a magnet for climbers, skiers, and tourists from all over the world.

As more and more rock is plucked from the bedrock sides and floor at the head of a glacier valley, the original depression gets larger and larger. The glacier carves a bowl-like hollow from the face of the mountain. Scientists call these bowls *cirques*, but they remind me of the stands in a baseball stadium. If two cirques are formed next to each other, a jagged ridge, an *arête*, is all that's left of the mountain mass between them. The pointed Taku Towers we're headed for are horns. These and other horns are formed when three or more glaciers carve cirques from different sides of the same land mass, leaving only a pointed peak. The Matterhorn in Switzerland is the most famous horn in the world.

The clouds have fully lifted now, and I guess we're only half an hour from camp.

If we were in a **deglaciated** area, we would also see cirques, moraines, and arêtes. Any place a glacier has traveled is usually covered with glacial drift. The soils and ground moraines that cover the plains of Iowa and other midwestern states and Manhattan Island were carried there by glaciers.

We know that some of the truck-size boulders in New York City's Central Park were carried hundreds of miles by the power of ice. Such boulders are called erratics.

Valleys carved by glaciers have a certain shape. While a V-shaped valley is made by a river, a U-shaped one is the work of a glacier. Yosemite Valley in California and the valleys in the White Mountains of New Hampshire are good examples of U-shaped, glacier-carved valleys.

deglaciated, deglaciation   melting away of ice and uncovering of earth during a warming period

(top) A small village in the Swiss Alps is nestled in a U-shaped valley carved by glaciers.

(bottom) In Alaska, four camp huts are perched safely on the side of a **nunatak**, sheltered from the vicious northern winds.

Amy's up in front talking with Matthew about the latest climbing gear, and I just heard you telling Yvette, the **geobotanist**, how much you'd love to crawl into your own warm bed tonight and sleep forever!

Finally, we see our camp, perched on the hillside about 1000 **meters** ahead. The aluminum roofs of our huts reflect the orange and pink sunset, a beautiful sight after all these hours of skiing. Welcome-home shouts come down from the camp, and we're greeted by people offering to carry our packs up the **nunatak**. Robin serves up the hot soup. We forget our blisters and backaches while we slurp our soup and talk about our journey. Then it's straight to bed in our aluminum-covered wooden huts. Tomorrow's going to be another long day, and sleep is essential to survival up here on the icefield.

When Jack, the camp manager, comes to waken us the next morning, I feel as though I'd shut my eyes just two minutes ago. You groan, roll over, and hide in your sleeping bag. He mentions breakfast, and we become more interested in getting out of bed.

We get up, wash in a bucket of ice-cold water, dress, and go to breakfast. Everyone takes turns doing the cooking, dishwashing, and other chores on an **expedition**. And you take care of your own gear, because there aren't any moms around to pick up after you—nor are there department stores where you can buy socks to replace the ones you've lost. On this icefield your gear is what keeps you alive!

geobotanist	one who studies plants in relation to geological formations
meter	metric measure of distance or length—1 meter = 39.37 inches
nunatak	(say, "noon attack") Eskimo for "mountain peaks that stick up above the surrounding glacial ice"
expedition	journey involving several people wanting to explore or accomplish a particular thing such as studying a glacier

(top) Here comes the helicopter with mail and supplies!

(bottom) You call this summer?

ALL IN A DAY'S WORK

After breakfast, Jack assigns us to camp jobs. Since the nunatak escaped yesterday's snowfall, Robin is sent down to the glacier to fill more buckets with snow to melt for the day's water supply. You and I are assigned to tighten the cables that anchor the huts to the ground. Without cables, the huts could be blown away by the constant strong winds around here. Everyone hears Todd grumble when he's assigned to clean the outhouse.

Soon we hear the approach of a helicopter. When it hovers above us, we whoop it up. It means mail call and supplies. It also means four or five trips down to the glacier and about 500 feet back up the nunatak to get them up to camp. The work is hard, but when it's done that long-awaited mail is given out!

The day's schedule is announced at mail call. We are to go fill our **daypacks** for our afternoon field work. Then we are to return to the main hut for a quick lecture by Yvette on plant and animal life on the nunatak and glacier.

You've been assigned to go with the **surveying crew**, while I go out with the **snow-pit** diggers. Poor Linda is stuck back at camp to be the radio "met" person who takes **meteorological readings** every three hours. The "met" person is also in charge of all radio communications for the day and helps the cook as well!

daypack	small, soft pack with room for things needed on a hike that doesn't require overnight supplies
surveying crew	in this case, a group that uses instruments to measure glacial movement
snow-pit	hole dug in the glacier to study layers of snow and ice
meteorological ("met") readings	reading of instruments that measure factors related to weather and climate such as wind speed, dewpoint, temperature

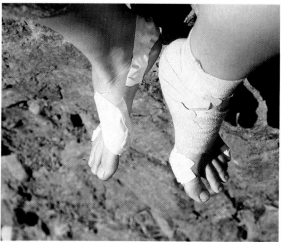

(top) In a zone full of **crevasses**, we use **ice axes** to probe for hollow spots. After a deep snow, crevasses could be hidden anywhere!

(bottom) Irreplaceable equipment: your body! Resident doctors hope for healing because there are no department stores selling new feet.

SURVIVAL

As we stuff our daypacks, I remember those first few days of introductory lectures. The staff told us that on any research expedition in a physically hostile environment, survival must come before science. On this expedition, 60 percent of all our efforts goes toward surviving. Cotton clothing is worthless because when it gets wet, it stays wet, and you'll freeze. Wool clothes keep you warmer and drier than anything else you can take.

Everyone packs the same basic survival gear: a wool cap, gloves, and sweater, rain pants and jacket, first aid kit, rope, and an **ice axe**. You even need a sunscreen. If the approaching blizzard doesn't freeze you, the sun reflecting off the snow at this 7500' altitude will burn you to a crisp. You also throw in your **crampons** and emergency ropes for walking in areas covered by **crevasses**. I always throw in my shorts for when the digging makes me too hot and sweaty for wool pants.

None of us was allowed to start this expedition without fully understanding the dangers of the places to be traveled. Here on the icefield we watch especially for crevasses by probing with our long-handled ice axes as we walk. We also have to know the symptoms and take special precautions to avoid **hypothermia** and **frostbite**.

ice axe	very pointed axe used in mountain climbing and travel across ice
crampons	footwear with spikes that dig into ice or snow to give a good footing
crevasse	very deep crack in the ice caused by pressures and stresses
hypothermia	condition when body temperature drops below normal; can result in death
frostbite	partial freezing of some part of the body due to loss of blood circulation; can mean loss of toes or other body parts

Moss Campion

Alpine SaxiFrage

Frail beauties hide from the harsh climate among the rocks.
They survive by growing very low, sometimes in clusters.

PLANTS AND ANIMALS

After we've finished packing, it's time for Yvette's lecture. As a geobotanist, she spends most of her time studying what little plant life manages to survive in this "deep freeze." Today she talks about the plant and animal life found around this one of twelve camps.

A thin layer of soil on the nunatak provides a **habitat** for low-growing bushes, willows, and even some wild flowers.

Very few animals can survive on the ice. Still, you may get your toe caught in a mousetrap if you're not careful. The mice that get to the icefield are probably stowaways from some supply box flown to the camp. They manage to survive nicely by stealing our food and cuddling up in someone's sock.

What else lives on the icefield besides a few mice? You look carefully at the snowfields and see that they're not flat but covered with small bowl-shaped **suncups**. A closer look reveals little black bugs crawling around on pinkish snow. The pink coloring is caused by billions of tiny **algae** that live with the little black **snow fleas** and **iceworms** in the snow and ice.

Yvette's lecture gets us even more excited about our daily "treasure hunt" for the mysteries of nature surrounding us in this majestic place.

habitat	living space that supplies the needs of an animal or plant
suncup	cup-like depressions on the ice and snow where sun *seems* to have had more chance to melt the surface
algae	plants with no specific roots, stems, or leaves; includes single-celled plants and seaweeds
snow flea	insect the size of a pinhead, adapted to life in the snow
iceworms	tiny dark worms (1—3cm long) that live at freezing point temperatures—They burrow into ice when air temperature is a few degrees above or below 0°C or 32°F.

Our snow-pit may have to be as deep as 20 feet before we reach last year's snow level. It takes teamwork. We pass the snow up to a person who passes it to another person, then another, and finally out of the pit.

Yvette explains that some plants and animals tell us how long it has been since a glacier covered the area being studied. Certain types of **lichen** on the nunatak rocks tell us the same thing. Scientists know the types of lichen and how fast they grow. By measuring the largest **diameters** of these lichens, they can estimate how long the lichen have been alive and thus how long since the glacier melted away.

After the lecture, it's time to go into the field. We're divided into groups of two to eight. Many of us are assistants, and as you have found, there's not much glamour in what we do. Today I have to go out with seven other assistants to dig a snow-pit. We dig down into the glacier until we reach last year's snow level. That means 15 to 20 feet of digging before we get to a thick layer of ice or dirty, grainy snow which we know is last year's snow level. This dirty layer has been caused by months of summer melting along with deposits of dust, **pollen**, or other fine material carried by winds. The ice layers were caused by meltwater refrozen by autumn's chilly wind. We may have to dig for three to eight hours. But luckily, in summer two-thirds of the top layer of snow is already melted. What if we had to dig 60-foot pits!

With shovels, ice axes, and determination, we dig for hours to make a snow-pit. We then measure the temperature and **density** of the ice every ten **centimeters** until we reach last year's layer of ice.

lichen	plant which is a combination of algae and fungi that grow very slowly on rocks and bark or dead wood
diameter	length of a straight line drawn from edge to edge through the center of a circle
pollen	powdery substance in flowers which is part of plant reproduction
density	compactness
centimeter (c)	metric measure: 1 inch = 2.54 centimeters

Blue ice at the terminus of the Mendenhall Glacier. Blue color is the result of lack of air in the ice after years of compaction at the glacier's base.

ANATOMY OF A GLACIER

The anatomy of glaciers is fascinating. A mound of fresh snow is composed of 90 percent air space, because snow falls in delicate, six-sided, star-shaped crystals. The weight of more snow compacts the crystals and makes the snow **denser**. Warm summer weather melts some of the ice and snow. The resulting meltwater **percolates** down through the snow and further compacts and **recrystallizes** it into what we call **firn** before it becomes very dense glacial ice. More air is squeezed out as the ice thickens. Crystals at the very bottom of glaciers have been squashed so much that they don't reflect as much white light as the air-filled crystals did. Because they are denser, these crystals reflect only the blue wavelength of light. This creates the beautiful clear blue ice seen at the very bottom of glaciers.

Glaciologists talk about a **glacial budget** in words like *advancing, receding*, and *equilibrium*. If a glacier accumulates more snow and ice than it loses by melting, or **ablation**, it thickens and *advances*. If it loses more mass than it gains, it gets thinner, smaller, and is said to *recede*. When a glacier has a "balanced budget," the increase in new snow is balanced out by the melting of old snow, or firn, during the summer. Such a glacier neither advances nor recedes. It's in a state of *equilibrium*.

denser	more compact
percolate	filter through
recrystallize	to turn from melted snow back into crystals or from snow crystals into ice crystals
firn	ice of intermediate density
glacial budget	accounting for loss, increase, and overall supply of snow that makes up a glacier
ablation	wasting away of a glacier by melting and evaporation

Snow-pit work is cold and tedious, but the smallest measurement is a big contribution toward the advancement of our understanding of glaciers.

All this information helps us understand the anatomy of the glacier, what it's actually like beneath the surface. It helps us know exactly how much snow fell during the previous year and how much has melted. We can also see channels where meltwater has percolated through the snow and refrozen. This gives us some understanding of the relationship between freezing and melting within the ice and why glaciers behave as they do.

As we continue digging and measuring, I notice that Robin's lips are a little bit blue and she seems really tired. I ask her if she's cold and she just turns to me, says nothing, and shivers without control. It looks like the beginning of hypothermia to me. This can be dangerous without immediate care. We aren't too far from camp, so I tell Todd to ski back with her. The skiing should warm her up. If she was truly hypothermic, we would have to warm her up at the snow-pit and have a crew from camp come out with hot liquid, extra clothes, and an **over-snow vehicle** to take her back.

The rest of us can't stop taking measurements. The snow conditions will change overnight, and the area exposed by our digging will also change and make our **data** worthless.

We're done soon enough and have a great ski back to camp after a gratifying day's work in the field. I ask about Robin and learn that the ski back to camp got her blood circulating enough to warm her up. And hot chocolate warms the rest of us while we discuss the day's work.

over-snow vehicle	large vehicle with treads like those of a military tank, used to travel across snow
data	measurements or other factual information used as a basis to develop scientific theories

(top) This instrument measures sunshine duration by magnifying the sun's rays enough to burn a line on paper behind it. At day's end, we have a record of how much or how little sunshine we got that day.

(bottom) Over-snow vehicle: important for transport of supplies and essential to any necessary rescues.

"MET" READINGS

I notice you're with Linda, who's talking on the radio to another trail party coming into camp. Her job as met-person is one of the most important. From 7:00 A.M. to 10:00 P.M., met people from all the twelve camps on the icefield take meteorological readings every three hours, talk on the radio three times a day to order supplies, and keep track of anyone out in the field. Even though the radio is for official use only, Linda gets the latest "leftovers recipe" for our fifth night of canned creamed chicken. Unfortunately, all the good food was dropped off by the helicopter at another camp!

The met person records information vital to the expedition's scientific success. The list includes temperatures, **visibility**, sunshine duration, present weather, **precipitation**, depth of newly-fallen snow, and types and amount of cloud cover. It takes only about 10 minutes to get all this data, but it's important to get it exactly the way the instruments record it.

At the end of the expedition, scientists will gather all of this information and compare it with that of other years. They'll look for climatic trends, cycles, and **anomalies** that will help us understand how the budget of these mighty glaciers reacts to even the most minor climatic changes.

visibility	how far it is possible to see
precipitation	amount of water that has fallen in the form of rain, snow, fog, hail, and sleet
anomalies	different and unexpected events or data

(top) An **ice fall**.

(bottom) Surveying crew gets instructions at the foot of the ice fall.

MEASURE FOR MEASURE

Today you went with a group to measure the movement of the **ice fall** just south of camp. You and four others were roped together as you traveled across the ice to avoid falling into deep cracks called *crevasses*. These slits open at the glacier's surface where the ice and snow are brittle. They crack under stress, just like dried-up, old rubber. About 100 feet deeper down, the ice acts more like new rubber as the glacier moves over a hump in the valley floor or some other obstacle. This ice is **elastic** and doesn't form crevasses.

When your group reached the ice fall, two of you climbed up as far as it was safe to go, and set up glass **prisms** in key places.

I remember when one of the scientists taught us to use the **EDM**, the **electronic distance measuring** instrument. He said it sends electronic signals like radio waves to the prisms. The signals are reflected from the prisms to the EDM, which then automatically computes the distance between them. By recording these distances over periods of time, you can tell just how fast a glacier is moving. Your group measured an ice fall where the glacier usually moves rapidly, so your day sounds more exciting than mine spent in the snow-pits. You even saw and heard some big **avalanches** within and on the sides of the ice fall as you recorded the information.

ice fall	part of a glacier that flows very slowly over a huge cliff
elastic	stretchable, pliable, springy
prism	wedge-shaped glass that bends beams of light
EDM, electronic distance measurer	instrument used to help measure the movement of a glacier
avalanche	rapid, violent movement of snow, ice, or other material down a slope

A midnight sunset to remember!

THE ROAR AND THE QUIET

After eight weeks of skiing from one camp to another and doing every job there is to do on an expedition, it's time to pack up and go home. We think about the summer's experience.

Through our field work and trail party travels we have seen real evidence of the treasures and powers of this mystifying icefield. I've learned to ignore blisters, and you're even starting to enjoy mushy peanut butter and jelly sandwiches. But more importantly, you and I and all the other research assistants have helped senior scientists to unlock some of the secrets hidden in the glaciers of the Juneau Icefield.

Without our surveying, met readings, communications, and digging of countless snow-pits, this expedition would not have been successful. Without scientists teaching us what they've learned in the past, student scientists could not continue these studies and develop new theories. The days go quickly, but each one brings us closer to the answers to all those questions about the world as it was, is, and may be tomorrow.

Sometimes the going got pretty rough and you couldn't wait to get back home. But now you know that once you get back to the roar of civilization, you'll be looking forward to next summer. You'll want to get back to the icefield where you'll hear another roar, that of the blizzard that threatens to blow over the shelters. But then there's the quiet of a midnight sunset and those ever-present questions about the POWER OF ICE.

GLOSSARY

ablation	wasting away of a glacier by melting and evaporation
advancing	growing — A glacier *advances* due to an increased amount of snow in the area of accumulation
algae	plants with no specific roots, stems, or leaves; includes single-celled plants and seaweeds
alpine glacier	mountain glacier formed and advancing through a pre-existing valley
anomalies	different and unexpected events or data
arête	mountain ridge formed when two glaciers carve opposite sides of a mountain
avalanche	rapid, violent movement of snow, ice, or other material down a slope
backpack	large, compartmented bag held on a sturdy frame to carry sleeping bag and other camping equipment
base camp	station where groups can live temporarily and go out to explore and/or do research
botanist	scientist who studies plants
centimeter (c)	metric measure: 1 inch = 2.54 centimeters
chemist	scientist who studies properties of substances, how they are put together, and how they react with each other
cirque	hollow area gouged out of the side of a mountain by a glacier shaped like half of a bowl
compass bearing	reading of a compass; needle points north and helps you determine which way you want to go
continental glacier	ice sheet that covers a large part of a continent and moves out in all directions from a central region of accumulation
crampons	footwear with spikes that dig into ice or snow to give a good footing
crevasse	very deep crack in the ice caused by pressures and stresses
data	measurements or other factual information used as a basis to develop scientific theories
daypack	small, soft pack with room for things needed on a hike that doesn't require overnight supplies
debris	loose fragments of rock, earth, and other materials

deglaciated, deglaciation	melting away of ice and uncovering of earth during a warming period
dendrochronologist	one who studies tree rings for the purposes of dating past events and understanding ancient climates
denser	more compact
density	compactness
diameter	length of a straight line drawn from edge to edge through the center of a circle
drift ice	ice on water broken up by winds and currents
EDM, electronic distance measurer	instrument used to help measure the movement of a glacier
elastic	stretchable, pliable, springy
equilibrium	a state of balance between opposing forces
erode	wear away
expedition	journey involving several people wanting to explore or accomplish a particular thing such as studying a glacier
firn	ice of intermediate density
force of gravity	attraction of bodies toward the center of the earth
frostbite	partial freezing of some part of the body due to loss of blood circulation; can mean loss of toes or other body parts
geobotanist	one who studies plants in relation to geological formations
geologist	earth scientist; one who studies the earth and the rocks of which it is formed
glacial budget	accounting for loss, increase, and overall supply of snow that makes up a glacier
glacial drift	combination of rocks, boulders, and finely ground rock caused by action of glaciers—See page 19.
glacial flour	rock ground to a fine powder by a glacier—See page 19.
glaciations	growth and outward spreading of glaciers over a period of time
glacier	mass of ice with limited width and direction of movement
glaciologist	scientist who studies glaciers
glaciology	study of glaciers

Great Ice Age	most recent cycle of glaciations, believed to have lasted 2.5 million years—See page 17.
habitat	living space that supplies the needs of an animal or plant
hydroelectric power	electricity generated by the force of flowing water
hypothermia	condition when body temperature drops below normal; can result in death
hypothesize	give ideas as possible explanations of something
ice age	span of geologic time, usually 1—3 million years, when the earth has had alternating warm and cold climates and been alternately covered and uncovered by glaciers—See *Great Ice Age.*
ice axe	very pointed axe used in mountain climbing and travel across ice
iceberg	huge mass of ice broken from a glacier, often found floating in water
icecap	constant, dome-shaped covering of ice and snow, especially those at the North and South Poles
ice fall	part of a glacier that flows very slowly over a huge cliff
icefields	large areas of land covered by different glaciers and areas of snow and ice accumulation
ice sheet	See *continental glacier.*
iceworms	tiny dark worms (1—3cm long) that live at freezing point temperatures—They burrow into ice when air temperature is a few degrees above or below 0°C or 32°F
lateral moraines	moraines pushed on the sides of a glacier—See *moraines* and page 19.
lichen	plant which is a combination of algae and fungi that grow very slowly on rocks and bark or dead wood
medial moraine	huge continuous mound of rocks and dirt formed between two parallel glaciers coming together
meltwater	any water melted from snow or ice
meteorological ("met") readings	reading of instruments that measure factors related to weather and climate such as wind speed, dewpoint, temperature
meter	metric measure of distance or length—1 meter = 39.37 inches
moraines	continuous mounds of dirt, rock, and debris pushed and piled up by a glacier along its sides and its terminus—See page 19.

nunatak	(say, "noon attack") Eskimo for "mountain peaks that stick up above surrounding glacial ice"
over-snow vehicle	large vehicle with treads like those of a military tank, used to travel across snow
percolate	filter through
physicist	scientist who studies matter, energy, motion, and force, and the laws of nature that affect how things work
pollen	powdery substance in flowers which is part of plant reproduction
precipitation	amount of water that has fallen in the form of rain, snow, fog, hail, and sleet
prism	wedge-shaped glass that bends beams of light
receding	melting of a glacier which makes the glacier appear to pull back or *recede*, especially when an alpine glacier seems to move back up the valley down which it had traveled
recrystallize	to turn from melted snow back into crystals or from snow crystals into ice crystals
snow flea	insect the size of a pinhead, adapted to life in the snow
snow-pit	hole dug in the glacier to study layers of snow and ice
stress fractures	cracks or breaks caused by pressure
suncup	cup-like depressions on the ice and snow where sun *seems* to have had more chance to melt the surface
surveying crew	in this case, a group that uses instruments to measure glacial movement
terminal moraine	mound of debris pushed and piled up by a glacier in front of itself—See *moraines.*
terminus	front of the glacier
trail party	group of people out on the trail away from camp for any purpose
unsorted soils	soils composed of mixtures of rock sizes from clays to gravels
valley glacier	See *alpine glacier.*
visibility	how far it is possible to see
whiteout	weather condition in which you are actually standing in clouds on the snow and you can't see where you are

INDEX

THE AUTHORS

At the ages of 17 and 18, **Lisa Sue Gitkin** (shown on page 18) joined the glaciological research expedition on the Juneau Icefields led by Dr. Maynard Miller of the University of Idaho. As a research assistant, Gitkin had experiences similar to those described in this book.

As an undergraduate at Stanford University, she spent a semester in France at the *Ecole des Mines* and *Ecole des Sciences Politique*. Vacations during that time were spent traveling around Europe, visiting the U.S.S.R., and skiing with a French ski team at Val d'Isere.

Graduating from Stanford with a degree in Applied Earth Sciences, Lisa Sue hopes to work in international economics and resource development.

Ruth Radlauer has written of glaciers before. As the author of 20 books about the national parks, she has studied glaciers at Olympic, Denali, and Glacier National Parks. She says, "It's almost impossible to write about the shape of the earth in the Northern Hemisphere without recording the visit of a glacier. There are the glacier-carved, U-shaped valleys in Yosemite, the once submerged islands of Acadia National Park, and evidence of glaciation as far south as the Indiana/Kentucky border.

Ruth and her husband, Ed Radlauer, are the authors of more than 200 books ranging in subjects from Volcanoes to Gymnastics, and Drag Racing to Dolls. They live in La Habra Heights, and Idyllwild, California.